North Africa

Ben Nussbaum

Consultants

William O'Mara, Ph.D.
History Professor
California State University, Dominguez Hills

Jon Anger
English, History, and ELD Teacher
Novato Unified School District

Publishing Credits

Rachelle Cracchiolo, M.S.Ed., *Publisher*
Emily R. Smith, M.A.Ed., *SVP of Content Development*
Véronique Bos, *Vice President of Creative*
Dani Neiley, *Editor*
Fabiola Sepulveda, *Series Graphic Designer*

Image Credits: p.4 Shutterstock/La bionda sulla Honda; p.12 (top) Shutterstock/Prin Adulyatham; p.13 Alamy/Gordon Sinclair; p.15 (top) Alamy/Lebrecht Music & Arts; p.17 (bottom) Alamy/Issam Elhafti; p.19 Alamy/Andreas Zeitler; p.20 Alamy/The Print Collector; p.22 (bottom) iStock/Numbeos; p.23 Shutterstock/MidoSemsem; p.24 Newscom/Mohamed Khidir/Xinhua News Agency; p.26 (top) Alamy/Andrea Forlani; p.27 (bottom) Alamy/Frans Lemmens; all other images from iStock and/or Shutterstock

Library of Congress Cataloging-in-Publication Data

Names: Nussbaum, Ben, 1975- author.
Title: North Africa / Ben Nussbaum.
Description: Huntington Beach : Teacher Created Materials, Inc, 2023. | Includes index. | Audience: Ages 8-18 | Summary: "North Africa has ancient pyramids-and modern factories. Huge cities sit by the Nile River and the Mediterranean Sea. There are also vast areas of empty desert. North Africa is a complex and changing region"-- Provided by publisher.
Identifiers: LCCN 2022038422 (print) | LCCN 2022038423 (ebook) | ISBN 9781087695167 (paperback) | ISBN 9781087695327 (ebook)
Subjects: LCSH: Africa, North--Juvenile literature.
Classification: LCC DT162 .N87 2023 (print) | LCC DT162 (ebook) | DDC 961--dc23/eng/20220817
LC record available at https://lccn.loc.gov/2022038422
LC ebook record available at https://lccn.loc.gov/2022038423

Shown on the cover is Aït Benhaddou in Morocco.

TCM | Teacher Created Materials

5482 Argosy Avenue
Huntington Beach, CA 92649
www.tcmpub.com
ISBN 978-1-0876-9516-7
© 2023 Teacher Created Materials, Inc.

Table of Contents

oasis in Libya

Travel to North Africa

North Africa has lush rivers and amazing beaches. It also has areas of vast, empty desert. It has monuments from thousands of years ago. And it has huge, modern factories. North Africa's history is rich in kingdoms and empires. But the lines on a map that divide its countries are fairly new.

It's important to note that North Africa does not have a single, accepted definition. But typically, North Africa stretches from Egypt in the east to Western Sahara in the west. The United Nations includes Sudan in North Africa. These countries all have long and complex histories. Islam is a common religion. Arabic is spoken across the region.

The countries share some challenges, too. They are all emerging from a time when Europe controlled North Africa. Protests in North Africa for better governments have inspired the world.

Cairo, Egypt

woman selling spices and nuts in a Moroccan market

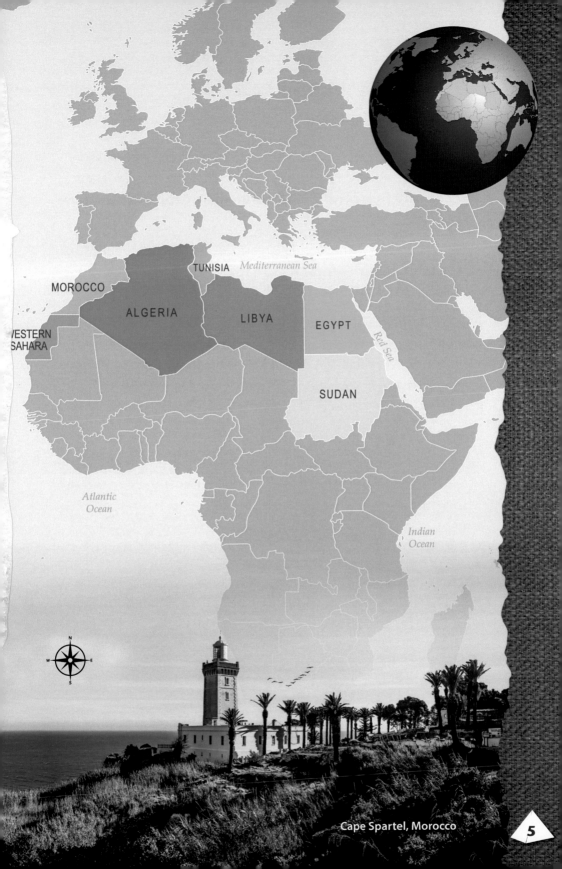

MOROCCO

TUNISIA

Mediterranean Sea

ALGERIA

LIBYA

EGYPT

WESTERN
SAHARA

Red Sea

SUDAN

*Atlantic
Ocean*

*Indian
Ocean*

N
W   E
S

Cape Spartel, Morocco

Desert, Water, and Mountains

North African countries are known for their sweeping, dry deserts as well as their lush, green landscapes. The geography of North Africa plays a huge role in where people live and how they live.

The Sahara is the world's largest desert. It takes up most of the land in North Africa. It has a total area of more than 3.3 million square miles (5.3 million square kilometers)!

In some places in the Sahara, there are beautiful mountains. In others, giant sand dunes shift and blow in the wind. Some places are very flat. No one lives in certain parts of the desert due to the heat. In other places, there are some homes.

These sandstone cliffs formed in the Sahara Desert in Algeria.

oasis in Libya

The Berber people have lived in and around the Sahara for thousands of years. The Tuareg people are one ethnic group within the Berbers. The Tuareg are known for being experts at surviving in the desert. For hundreds of years, they have led huge **caravans** through the Sahara. The caravans carried goods, such as gold, salt, and **ivory**, across the desert.

To make it through the Sahara, the Tuareg relied on oases. There are about 90 major oases in the Sahara. An oasis is a place in the desert where water emerges from deep underground to form a pond or lake.

Another group of Berber people is the Kabyle. They live in the northern part of Algeria. In the late 20th century, there were two million of them.

Diverse Languages

Berber man

The languages people speak in North Africa vary across the land. Arabic is spoken by many North Africans. This language has many dialects. The written language has differences from the spoken language. Students learn modern literary Arabic in school. There are also many Berber languages. Today, Berber languages are spoken by around 14 million people.

Atlas Mountains in Morocco

North Africa is not all desert. Other than Sudan and Western Sahara, all the countries of North Africa touch the Mediterranean Sea. This sea is mostly gentle, calm, and warm.

For thousands of years, this sea has been a body of water connecting Europe, the Middle East, and North Africa. This means that North Africa has been a place where many languages, religions, and cultures have mixed together for a very long time.

The Mediterranean Sea benefits North Africa in another way. Clouds carry moisture in from the water. In Morocco, Algeria, and Tunisia, the Atlas Mountains trap the clouds. The moisture from the clouds is kept between the sea and the mountains.

view of the Mediterranean Sea from Annaba, Algeria

This area between the sea and the mountains has a climate that some people would say is perfect. It is not too warm in the summer or too cold in the winter. It's mild, and crops can grow throughout the entire year. This stretch of land is not very big. In some places, it is about 100 miles (161 kilometers) wide. In other places, it is much less. This area is filled with homes and businesses. Many of the biggest cities in North Africa are in this area.

Close Neighbors!

The Strait of Gibraltar is where North Africa is closest to Europe. One side of the strait borders Morocco, which is part of Africa. The other borders Spain, which is part of Europe. They are separated by only about 8 miles (13 kilometers).

Spain

Strait of Gibraltar

Morocco

Another important part of the geography of North Africa is the Nile River. It is one of the world's longest rivers. It begins in Uganda in central Africa and flows north toward the Mediterranean. The eastern part of North Africa is heavily influenced by the Nile River.

The Nile is at its strongest in Egypt. Egyptian cities have flourished on the banks of the Nile for a very long time. Today, most Egyptians live within a short distance of the Nile.

In an otherwise dry land, the Nile provides water for drinking and for crops. Water from the Nile is used for **irrigation**. It is brought into fields through pipes. Dams on the Nile provide **hydroelectric** power and control the flow of water.

Before the dams were built, the Nile flooded each year, creating a wide, swampy area. The floods lasted for several months. These floods were very important for Egyptian farmers. The floods created great farmland. They left behind moist soil that was rich in **nutrients**.

The Nile is also very important for travel. For thousands of years, ships loaded with copper, iron, grain, and more have traveled up and down the Nile. They carry necessary building materials and food.

The Nile River flows through Cairo,
Egypt's capital city.

The Longest River

There is some debate about which river is
the longest in the world. It is either the
Nile River or the Amazon River, which
is in South America. It is not easy to
measure how long a river is. A river curves
and changes shape, so it is hard to know
exactly where a river starts and ends.

satellite view of
the Nile River

A Proud History

The Nile has played a big role in the history of North Africa—and the world. About 5,000 years ago, a ruler took control of several cities on the Nile. He was the first **pharaoh** to reign over Upper and Lower Egypt. He was known as Narmer or Menes. His reign marked the start of the Egyptian kingdom.

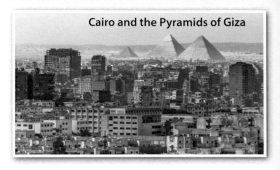
Cairo and the Pyramids of Giza

The Egyptian kingdom lasted in one form or another for about 3,000 years. At different times, it grew or faded in power. But, it was always based around the Nile.

temple wall in Egypt

The ancient Egyptians invented new ways to build boats, write, and do mathematics. They left behind amazing structures and art. These include the Pyramids of Giza, the Sphinx, and other monuments.

Piles of Pyramids

More than 100 ancient pyramids have been located in Egypt. Most are small and were covered by sand before being rediscovered. Pyramids were used as tombs. Egyptian kings were buried in pyramids.

Step Pyramid of Djoser

illustration of
ancient Carthage

Another North African empire belonged to the city of
Carthage. This empire approached Egypt in terms of size and
wealth, but it is not nearly as famous today.

Carthage was founded almost 3,000 years ago by people
from the Middle East. They were known as the Phoenicians.
Carthage became very powerful because of trading. Ships from
Carthage went everywhere in the Mediterranean. They traded
goods, such as wood, clothing, spices, and precious metals.
They also sailed outside the Mediterranean. They went to
Britain and Nigeria.

ruins of Carthage

Carthage was huge. It stretched from the coast of North Africa to parts of modern-day Italy and Spain. After many bitter wars, Rome defeated Carthage. Today, Carthage is a **suburb** of the city of Tunis. It is full of expensive houses. But there are some ruins of ancient Carthage that can be visited.

The Vandals

Carthage was briefly ruled by a tribe called the Vandals. They came to North Africa from Europe, leaving destruction behind them. The modern word *vandal* comes from this tribe.

The next great empire in the history of North Africa came from the Middle East. It was founded on the religion of Islam. This religion started around 600 CE. Islam spread quickly. Inspired by this new religion, armies built caliphates. A caliphate is like a kingdom. Instead of being ruled by a king, it is ruled by a caliph. A caliph is considered the leader of the entire Muslim community.

Different caliphates ruled North Africa at different times. One caliphate created Egypt's first modern university around 970 CE. This university still exists! These caliphates lasted for hundreds of years. About 800 years ago, they were replaced by smaller countries. Some of these countries lasted for a long time. Some lasted for a very short period.

illustration of life during the Abbasid caliphate

Al-Azhar Mosque is well-known for being an Islamic learning center.

Economies and Industries

The countries of North Africa have similarities in terms of their **economies**. Some people work as farmers. Crops, such as olives and figs, grow well along the coast. Oranges and lemons are common crops, too.

Tourism is important. The weather and warm beaches draw visitors. North Africa's history also attracts people. Millions of tourists visit Egypt every year. Top attractions are the Pyramids of Giza and the Great Sphinx of Giza. In Tunisia and Libya, buildings from the Roman era bring in visitors. In cities such as Marrakesh, visitors walk down streets that are nearly 1,000 years old.

Marrakesh, Morocco

No Cars Here

In a few of North Africa's oldest cities, there are some neighborhoods where you cannot drive a car. The neighborhoods were built before cars existed, so they have very narrow streets. Marrakesh is one of these areas.

A fisherman sells his catch at a local market in Hurghada, Egypt.

car factory in Morocco

There are differences among the economies in these countries, too. Morocco's economy is one of the strongest in all of Africa. One reason is that it has a large fishing industry. Most of the boats from Morocco spend weeks at a time in the Atlantic Ocean. The fishers catch seafood, such as sardines and octopuses. Morocco also has a strong **automotive** industry. Many of the cars and trucks sold in Africa are made there.

Egypt's economy is also very strong. Egypt makes a lot of money from its manufactured goods. Fabric and clothing are big industries. Thousands of factories make clothing from cotton. Clothing is a major industry in Tunisia, too.

In Algeria, Libya, and Egypt, oil is an important part of the economy. Oil is turned into gasoline. It also can be turned into plastics and many other products. In Libya, the big **oil fields** are in the desert. Wells pull oil from deep underground. Then, pipelines carry the oil north to the coast. From there, it is shipped to other countries.

Most of the oil fields in Egypt are in or near the Gulf of Suez. This body of water is relatively small, but it is very important. This is because the Gulf of Suez is very rich in oil. On the gulf, huge platforms perch above the water. They drill for oil under the **seabed**. The Suez **Canal** is located at the north end of the gulf. It is important for trade in this region. The human-made canal connects the Mediterranean Sea and the Red Sea. Goods from around the world travel through this waterway.

oil drilling rig in the Gulf of Suez, Egypt

All That Oil

A lot of oil has been removed from the oil fields in Libya. But it is thought that about 48 billion barrels of oil are still there underground. By some estimates, the oil will run out in about 590 years.

Miners work in Morocco.

Algeria is one of the world's leaders in producing natural gas. Natural gas is not the same as gasoline used in cars. Natural gas is most often used for heating homes and water. Algeria's natural gas is used in North Africa or transported to Europe. It is carried by pipes that lie on the bottom of the Mediterranean Sea. Pipes also transport Algeria's oil to ports along the Mediterranean. From there, the oil is exported around the world.

In the western part of North Africa, mining is important. The Atlas Mountains are rich in minerals. These include phosphate, copper, and silver.

North Africa Today

North Africa has a rich history. However, in certain ways, the countries of North Africa are still emerging.

European countries controlled most of Africa until recently. In 1884, the major countries of Europe had a conference. It was in the city of Berlin, Germany. At this conference, they made many decisions. Most were about trade and slavery. They also decided which countries would control parts of Africa.

Most of North Africa gained independence in the 1950s and 1960s. One example is Algeria. In the past, France had control over Algeria. The French did not treat the Algerians well. Algerian schools were not good because there was not enough **funding**. The government was based on what was good for France, not Algeria.

Algerians fought for their independence. It took a long war. Many people died, and homes were destroyed. After eight years, the Algerians won. In 1962, they achieved independence.

It is hard to become an independent country. There are a lot of questions to answer. Who should be the leader? What is the best way to make important decisions? How can the country stay united? These questions had to be addressed.

The Algerian Army of Liberation drives down a street in 1962.

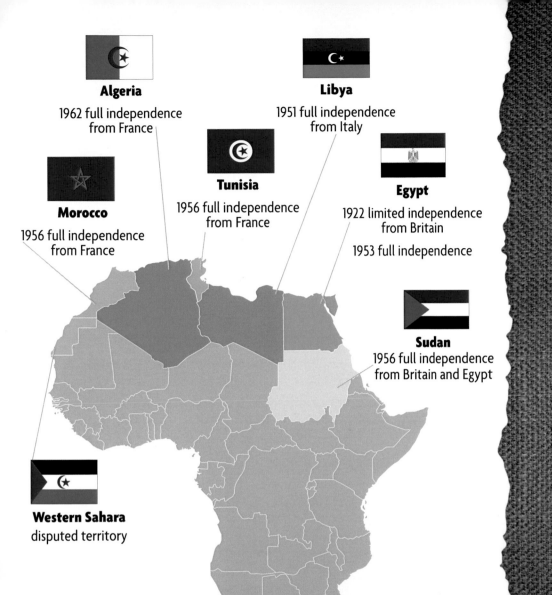

Algeria
1962 full independence
from France

Libya
1951 full independence
from Italy

Tunisia
1956 full independence
from France

Egypt
1922 limited independence
from Britain

1953 full independence

Morocco
1956 full independence
from France

Sudan
1956 full independence
from Britain and Egypt

Western Sahara
disputed territory

Africa's Map Is Still Changing

Sudan split in 2011 into Sudan and South Sudan.
Western Sahara is a **disputed** territory on the western
edge of the African continent. At least 80 percent
is controlled by Morocco. The other 20 percent is
controlled by the Sahrawi Arab Democratic Republic.
If Western Sahara becomes independent, Africa's
borders may change again.

In Algeria, a president took over when the country became independent. He was not very popular. A few years later, the military took control. The military has been heavily involved in Algeria ever since. People can vote, but the military must approve the candidates.

In Algeria, voters have their fingers marked with ink so they cannot vote twice.

In many African countries, people have taken steps to make changes. In 2011, Tunisians protested in huge numbers. They were unhappy with their government. Only two presidents had served between 1957 and 2011. The current president had been in power for 23 years. Because of the protests, he fled the country. Elections were held later.

torn poster of the Tunisian president

The change in Tunisia inspired people in other countries. Many leaders in North Africa were forced to step down. Some people call this revolution the Arab Spring. The Arab Spring did not solve all the problems of North Africa. There are still very important questions people are debating. One is about how to share wealth. Oil, natural gas, and mining bring in a lot of money. Companies pay the government to be able to drill or mine. What should the government do with the money? Sometimes, leaders keep some of it for themselves. They become rich. But this is not fair to the rest of the people in the countries. **Corruption** remains a big problem.

A Wealthy Leader

Muammar al-Qaddafi was the leader of Libya for 42 years from 1969 to 2011. During that time, he built a vast fortune by putting himself or his family in charge of big parts of the economy. This corruption was one reason he was overthrown.

23

People in Sudan attend a celebration ceremony in 2020 and wait for the government to sign a peace deal.

Another question that citizens debate is the role of religion. Most North Africans are Muslim. This brings up several questions. Should the governments base laws on Islam? If so, who gets to interpret Islam? Who should decide how to make laws based on it?

A government based on religion is called a **theocracy**. Sudan became a theocracy in 2011. This happened after years of fighting and a civil war. The laws were all based on Islamic teachings. Belonging to a different religion was illegal. But in 2020, Sudan stopped being a theocracy. Laws were changed to allow more freedom.

Qur'an

Water is another big issue on this dry continent. In North Africa, it can be a challenge to find enough water for farming and for people to drink and use. What one country does has an impact on other countries. For example, if Sudan uses more water from the Nile River, that means there is less water for Egypt.

Taking water from the ocean is one option. But ocean water is salty. It can be expensive to remove the salt, and it creates pollution. The salt that was taken out has to be disposed of somewhere. Figuring out the best water policies will be a huge factor in the future of North Africa.

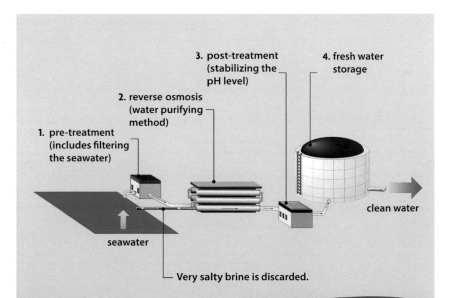

3. post-treatment (stabilizing the pH level)

4. fresh water storage

2. reverse osmosis (water purifying method)

1. pre-treatment (includes filtering the seawater)

clean water

seawater

Very salty brine is discarded.

Getting the Salt Out

The process of making ocean water usable for people is called *desalination*. Whether people should do it is a big debate in many places around the world. It is a very expensive process. It requires a lot of energy to remove the salt from ocean water.

A Fascinating Cup of Tea

In most places in North Africa, drinking tea is an important **ritual**. Families and friends gather to sip tea. As they sip, they may watch the sun set over the mountains or desert. Or maybe they watch ships sail the Nile or pull into a Mediterranean harbor. They may eat some sweet treats, including *deblah*. These are Tunisian pastries that are fried, covered in lemon syrup, and sprinkled with chopped nuts.

woman pouring tea in Morocco

Popular Desserts

In Egypt, *um ali* is a popular dessert that can be served with tea. It is usually made with bread, raisins, coconut, pistachios, and sugar. *Griouech* (also spelled *griwech*) is a type of fried pastry. It is made with orange blossom water. The pastries are dipped in honey and have sesame seeds on top.

um ali

griouech

People from different parts of North Africa enjoy different types of teas. For example, in northern Egypt, people prefer a light black tea. In southern Egypt, the tea is stronger and darker. In Algeria,

fresh mint is used to make tea. In Libya, the tea is so thick that it is syrupy. It is tradition to serve each person three cups of tea.

The rituals involved in preparing and serving tea show this region's value of community and family. They show how North Africans have many things in common. They also show how not all North Africans are the same. It is just one look into this beautiful and complex area. North Africa has endless layers of culture and history.

A Berber family has tea in Morocco.

Map It!

The Sahara Desert is huge. It takes up about 25 percent of the entire continent of Africa. The Sahara has a large range of different landscapes. It's also dotted with major oases. In Egypt and Sudan, huge cities are in the Sahara. They sit on the Nile River, which cuts through the desert. Create a map showcasing some landmarks in the Sahara.

1. Draw or print a map of the top half of Africa.

2. On your map, label the Atlas Mountains and the Nile River.

3. Add a label for the Great Sand Sea. This is the region of the Sahara with the most dramatic sand dunes.

4. Label at least 10 more major landmarks in the desert. You can research these on the internet or find them in books. These can be cities, oases, mountain ranges, or anything else you can think of.

5. Print pictures of each landmark to go alongside your map. Or you can create a slideshow of pictures of the landmarks.

Sahara Desert sand dunes

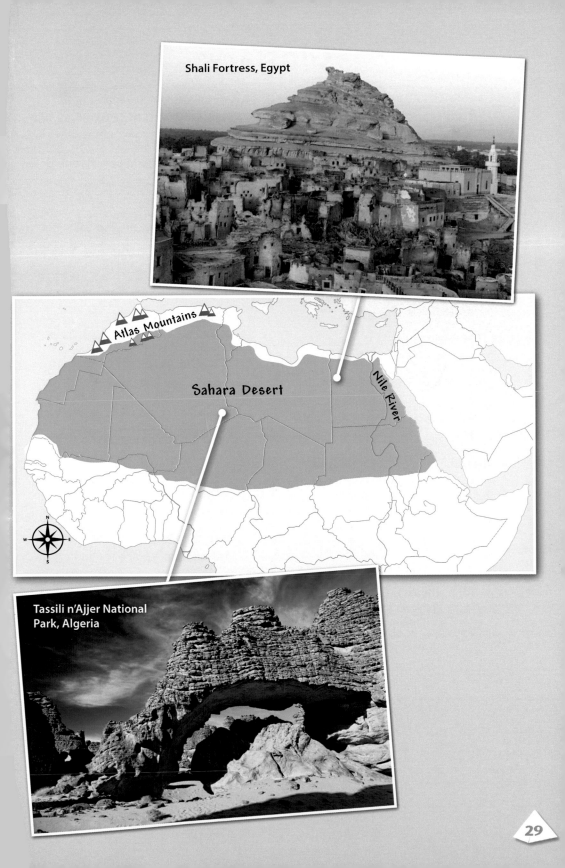

Shali Fortress, Egypt

Atlas Mountains

Sahara Desert

Nile River

Tassili n'Ajjer National Park, Algeria

Glossary

automotive—relating to cars or trucks

canal—a human-made waterway that allows boats or ships to pass

caravans—groups of people or animals traveling together, usually loaded with goods

corruption—dishonest or illegal behavior especially by people in positions of power

disputed—subject of controversy or contention

economies—the systems of making, selling, and buying goods and services in particular places

funding—an amount of money given by an organization for a specific purpose

hydroelectric—electricity created by moving water

irrigation—the method of supplying land with water by using artificial means (such as pipes)

ivory—hard, white material, typically from the tusk of an elephant

nutrients—substances that help people, animals, or plants grow and be healthy

oil fields—areas of land that have large amounts of oil under the ground

pharaoh—a ruler of ancient Egypt

ritual—an act that is regularly performed the same way

seabed—the bottom of a sea or ocean

suburb—a small town near a major city

theocracy—a government in which leaders guide based on religion

tourism—the practice of traveling to a place for fun or relaxation

a fortress in Rabat, Morocco

Index

Learn More!

Cleopatra is one of the most famous people in history. She was the last queen of the mighty Egyptian Empire. This empire lasted in one form or another for about 3,000 years.

Create a presentation about Cleopatra. Be sure to include information about the following people in her life:

- Ptolemy XII, her father
- Julius Caesar, a ruler of Rome
- Mark Antony, a Roman general

Include examples of how Cleopatra has been depicted over time. You should include pictures of sculptures and paintings of Cleopatra. You can also include depictions of Cleopatra from movies.

engraving of Cleopatra and her son on a temple wall in Egypt